LARGE PRINT ADDRESS BOOK

FOR LOW VISION

Frances P Robinson

THIS ADDRESS BOOK BELONGS TO

_____

IF FOUND PLEASE CALL

_____

Introduction

This Book was created specifically for those who have low vision capability and need a Large Print Address Book. Each page has a bold letter in the top corner to make the correct page of the alphabet easy to find.

Generous spacing of lines and bold text provide more than ample space for large letters or writing when entering information. When needed this information should be as easy as possible to read for those with diminished eyesight.

The front pages allow for doctor or emergency contacts to be entered so they can quickly be found if needed. The last pages of the large print address book include a section for notes.

DOCTORS and EMERGENCY

Name _____
Address _____
_____
Phone _____
_____

Name _____
Address _____
_____
Phone _____
_____

Name _____
Address _____
_____
Phone _____
_____

DOCTORS and EMERGENCY

Name_____
Address _____
_____
Phone _____
_____

Name_____
Address _____
_____
Phone _____
_____

Name_____
Address _____
_____
Phone _____
_____

DOCTORS and EMERGENCY

Name _____
Address _____
_____
Phone _____
_____

Name _____
Address _____
_____
Phone _____
_____

Name _____
Address _____
_____
Phone _____
_____

DOCTORS and EMERGENCY

Name _____
Address _____
_____
Phone _____
_____

Name _____
Address _____
_____
Phone _____
_____

Name _____
Address _____
_____
Phone _____
_____

DOCTORS and EMERGENCY

Name _____
Address _____
_____
Phone _____
_____

Name _____
Address _____
_____
Phone _____
_____

Name _____
Address _____
_____
Phone _____
_____

DOCTORS and EMERGENCY

Name_____
Address _____
_____
Phone _____
_____

Name_____
Address _____
_____
Phone _____
_____

Name_____
Address _____
_____
Phone _____
_____

A

Name_____
Address _____
_____
Phone _____
Cell _____

Name_____
Address _____
_____
Phone _____
Cell _____

Name_____
Address _____
_____
Phone _____
Cell _____

A

Name_____
Address _____
_____
Phone _____
Cell _____

Name_____
Address _____
_____
Phone _____
Cell _____

Name_____
Address _____
_____
Phone _____
Cell _____

Name _____
Address _____
_____
Phone _____
Cell _____

Name _____
Address _____
_____
Phone _____
Cell _____

Name _____
Address _____
_____
Phone _____
Cell _____

A

Name_____
Address _____
_____
Phone _____
Cell _____

Name_____
Address _____
_____
Phone _____
Cell _____

Name_____
Address _____
_____
Phone _____
Cell _____

A

Name_____
Address _____
_____
Phone _____
Cell _____

Name_____
Address _____
_____
Phone _____
Cell _____

Name_____
Address _____
_____
Phone _____
Cell _____

A

Name_____
Address _____
_____
Phone _____
Cell _____

Name_____
Address _____
_____
Phone _____
Cell _____

Name_____
Address _____
_____
Phone _____
Cell _____

Name_____
Address _____
_____
Phone _____
Cell _____

Name_____
Address _____
_____
Phone _____
Cell _____

Name_____
Address _____
_____
Phone _____
Cell _____

A

Name_____
Address _____
_____
Phone _____
Cell _____

Name_____
Address _____
_____
Phone _____
Cell _____

Name_____
Address _____
_____
Phone _____
Cell _____

B

Name_____
Address _____
_____
Phone _____
Cell _____

Name_____
Address _____
_____
Phone _____
Cell _____

Name_____
Address _____
_____
Phone _____
Cell _____

B

Name_____
Address _____
_____
Phone _____
Cell _____

Name_____
Address _____
_____
Phone _____
Cell _____

Name_____
Address _____
_____
Phone _____
Cell _____

B

Name_____
Address _____
_____
Phone _____
Cell _____

Name_____
Address _____
_____
Phone _____
Cell _____

Name_____
Address _____
_____
Phone _____
Cell _____

B

Name_____
Address
_____
_____
Phone _____
Cell _____

Name_____
Address
_____
_____
Phone _____
Cell _____

Name_____
Address
_____
_____
Phone _____
Cell _____

B

Name	_____
Address	_____
	_____
Phone	_____
Cell	_____

Name	_____
Address	_____
	_____
Phone	_____
Cell	_____

Name	_____
Address	_____
	_____
Phone	_____
Cell	_____

B

Name_____
Address _____
_____
Phone _____
Cell _____

Name_____
Address _____
_____
Phone _____
Cell _____

Name_____
Address _____
_____
Phone _____
Cell _____

Name_____
Address _____
_____
Phone _____
Cell _____

Name_____
Address _____
_____
Phone _____
Cell _____

Name_____
Address _____
_____
Phone _____
Cell _____

C

Name_____
Address _____

_____
Phone _____
Cell _____

Name_____
Address _____

_____
Phone _____
Cell _____

Name_____
Address _____

_____
Phone _____
Cell _____

Name _____
Address _____
_____
Phone _____
Cell _____

Name _____
Address _____
_____
Phone _____
Cell _____

Name _____
Address _____
_____
Phone _____
Cell _____

C

Name_____
Address _____
_____
Phone _____
Cell _____

Name_____
Address _____
_____
Phone _____
Cell _____

Name_____
Address _____
_____
Phone _____
Cell _____

Name_____
Address _____
_____
Phone _____
Cell _____

Name_____
Address _____
_____
Phone _____
Cell _____

Name_____
Address _____
_____
Phone _____
Cell _____

C

Name_____
Address _____
_____
Phone _____
Cell _____

Name_____
Address _____
_____
Phone _____
Cell _____

Name_____
Address _____
_____
Phone _____
Cell _____

D

Name_____

Address _____

_____

Phone _____

Cell _____

Name_____

Address _____

_____

Phone _____

Cell _____

Name_____

Address _____

_____

Phone _____

Cell _____

D

Name _____

Address _____

_____

Phone _____

Cell _____

Name _____

Address _____

_____

Phone _____

Cell _____

Name _____

Address _____

_____

Phone _____

Cell _____

D

Name_____
Address _____
_____
Phone _____
Cell _____

Name_____
Address _____
_____
Phone _____
Cell _____

Name_____
Address _____
_____
Phone _____
Cell _____

D

Name_____
Address _____
_____
Phone _____
Cell _____

Name_____
Address _____
_____
Phone _____
Cell _____

Name_____
Address _____
_____
Phone _____
Cell _____

D

Name _____
Address _____
_____
Phone _____
Cell _____

Name _____
Address _____
_____
Phone _____
Cell _____

Name _____
Address _____
_____
Phone _____
Cell _____

D

Name_____

Address _____

_____

Phone _____

Cell _____

Name_____

Address _____

_____

Phone _____

Cell _____

Name_____

Address _____

_____

Phone _____

Cell _____

Name_____
Address _____
_____
Phone _____
Cell _____

Name_____
Address _____
_____
Phone _____
Cell _____

Name_____
Address _____
_____
Phone _____
Cell _____

E

Name_____
Address _____

_____
Phone _____
Cell _____

Name_____
Address _____

_____
Phone _____
Cell _____

Name_____
Address _____

_____
Phone _____
Cell _____

E

Name_____
Address _____
_____
Phone _____
Cell _____

Name_____
Address _____
_____
Phone _____
Cell _____

Name_____
Address _____
_____
Phone _____
Cell _____

Name_____
Address _____
_____
Phone _____
Cell _____

Name_____
Address _____
_____
Phone _____
Cell _____

Name_____
Address _____
_____
Phone _____
Cell _____

Name_____
Address _____
_____
Phone _____
Cell _____

Name_____
Address _____
_____
Phone _____
Cell _____

Name_____
Address _____
_____
Phone _____
Cell _____

F

Name_____
Address _____
_____
Phone _____
Cell _____

Name_____
Address _____
_____
Phone _____
Cell _____

Name_____
Address _____
_____
Phone _____
Cell _____

F

Name_____
Address _____
_____
Phone _____
Cell _____

Name_____
Address _____
_____
Phone _____
Cell _____

Name_____
Address _____
_____
Phone _____
Cell _____

F

Name_____
Address _____
_____
Phone _____
Cell _____

Name_____
Address _____
_____
Phone _____
Cell _____

Name_____
Address _____
_____
Phone _____
Cell _____

Name_____
Address _____
_____
Phone _____
Cell _____

Name_____
Address _____
_____
Phone _____
Cell _____

Name_____
Address _____
_____
Phone _____
Cell _____

G

Name_____
Address _____

_____
Phone _____
Cell _____

Name_____
Address _____

_____
Phone _____
Cell _____

Name_____
Address _____

_____
Phone _____
Cell _____

Name_____
Address _____
_____
Phone _____
Cell _____

Name_____
Address _____
_____
Phone _____
Cell _____

Name_____
Address _____
_____
Phone _____
Cell _____

G

Name_____
Address _____
_____
Phone _____
Cell _____

Name_____
Address _____
_____
Phone _____
Cell _____

Name_____
Address _____
_____
Phone _____
Cell _____

Name_____
Address _____
_____
Phone _____
Cell _____

Name_____
Address _____
_____
Phone _____
Cell _____

Name_____
Address _____
_____
Phone _____
Cell _____

G

Name_____
Address _____
_____
Phone _____
Cell _____

Name_____
Address _____
_____
Phone _____
Cell _____

Name_____
Address _____
_____
Phone _____
Cell _____

Name_____
Address _____

_____
Phone _____
Cell _____

Name_____
Address _____

_____
Phone _____
Cell _____

Name_____
Address _____

_____
Phone _____
Cell _____

H

Name_____
Address _____
_____
Phone _____
Cell _____

Name_____
Address _____
_____
Phone _____
Cell _____

Name_____
Address _____
_____
Phone _____
Cell _____

Name_____

Address _____

_____

Phone _____

Cell _____

Name_____

Address _____

_____

Phone _____

Cell _____

Name_____

Address _____

_____

Phone _____

Cell _____

Name_____
Address _____
_____
Phone _____
Cell _____

Name_____
Address _____
_____
Phone _____
Cell _____

Name_____
Address _____
_____
Phone _____
Cell _____

Name_____

Address _____

_____

Phone _____

Cell _____

Name_____

Address _____

_____

Phone _____

Cell _____

Name_____

Address _____

_____

Phone _____

Cell _____

I

Name_____
Address _____
_____
Phone _____
Cell _____

Name_____
Address _____
_____
Phone _____
Cell _____

Name_____
Address _____
_____
Phone _____
Cell _____

Name_____

Address _____

_____

Phone _____

Cell _____

Name_____

Address _____

_____

Phone _____

Cell _____

Name_____

Address _____

_____

Phone _____

Cell _____

I

Name_____

Address _____

_____

Phone _____

Cell _____

Name_____

Address _____

_____

Phone _____

Cell _____

Name_____

Address _____

_____

Phone _____

Cell _____

Name_____

Address _____

_____

Phone _____

Cell _____

Name_____

Address _____

_____

Phone _____

Cell _____

Name _____

Address _____

_____

Phone _____

Cell _____

J

Name_____

Address _____

_____

Phone _____

Cell _____

Name_____

Address _____

_____

Phone _____

Cell _____

Name_____

Address _____

_____

Phone _____

Cell _____

J

Name_____
Address _____
_____
Phone _____
Cell _____

Name_____
Address _____
_____
Phone _____
Cell _____

Name_____
Address _____
_____
Phone _____
Cell _____

J

Name_____
Address _____
_____
Phone _____
Cell _____

Name_____
Address _____
_____
Phone _____
Cell _____

Name_____
Address _____
_____
Phone _____
Cell _____

K

Name_____
Address _____
_____
Phone _____
Cell _____

Name_____
Address _____
_____
Phone _____
Cell _____

Name_____
Address _____
_____
Phone _____
Cell _____

K

Name_____

Address _____

_____

Phone _____

Cell _____

Name_____

Address _____

_____

Phone _____

Cell _____

Name_____

Address _____

_____

Phone _____

Cell _____

Name_____

Address _____

_____

Phone _____

Cell _____

Name_____

Address _____

_____

Phone _____

Cell _____

Name_____

Address _____

_____

Phone _____

Cell _____

K

Name_____

Address _____

_____

Phone _____

Cell _____

Name_____

Address _____

_____

Phone _____

Cell _____

Name_____

Address _____

_____

Phone _____

Cell _____

L

Name _____
Address _____
_____
Phone _____
Cell _____

Name _____
Address _____
_____
Phone _____
Cell _____

Name _____
Address _____
_____
Phone _____
Cell _____

L

Name_____
Address _____
_____
Phone _____
Cell _____

Name_____
Address _____
_____
Phone _____
Cell _____

Name_____
Address _____
_____
Phone _____
Cell _____

L

Name _____
Address _____

_____
Phone _____
Cell _____

Name _____
Address _____

_____
Phone _____
Cell _____

Name _____
Address _____

_____
Phone _____
Cell _____

L

Name_____
Address _____
_____
Phone _____
Cell _____

Name_____
Address _____
_____
Phone _____
Cell _____

Name_____
Address _____
_____
Phone _____
Cell _____

L

Name _____
Address _____
_____
Phone _____
Cell _____

Name _____
Address _____
_____
Phone _____
Cell _____

Name _____
Address _____
_____
Phone _____
Cell _____

L

Name _____
Address _____
_____
Phone _____
Cell _____

Name _____
Address _____
_____
Phone _____
Cell _____

Name _____
Address _____
_____
Phone _____
Cell _____

M

Name_____
Address _____
_____
Phone _____
Cell _____

Name_____
Address _____
_____
Phone _____
Cell _____

Name_____
Address _____
_____
Phone _____
Cell _____

M

Name _____
Address _____
_____
Phone _____
Cell _____

Name _____
Address _____
_____
Phone _____
Cell _____

Name _____
Address _____
_____
Phone _____
Cell _____

Name_____
Address _____
_____
Phone _____
Cell _____

Name_____
Address _____
_____
Phone _____
Cell _____

Name_____
Address _____
_____
Phone _____
Cell _____

M

Name_____
Address _____
_____
Phone _____
Cell _____

Name_____
Address _____
_____
Phone _____
Cell _____

Name_____
Address _____
_____
Phone _____
Cell _____

M

Name_____
Address _____
_____
Phone _____
Cell _____

Name_____
Address _____
_____
Phone _____
Cell _____

Name_____
Address _____
_____
Phone _____
Cell _____

Name_____
Address _____
_____
Phone _____
Cell _____

Name_____
Address _____
_____
Phone _____
Cell _____

Name_____
Address _____
_____
Phone _____
Cell _____

N

Name_____

Address _____

_____

Phone _____

Cell _____

Name_____

Address _____

_____

Phone _____

Cell _____

Name_____

Address _____

_____

Phone _____

Cell _____

N

Name_____
Address _____
_____
Phone _____
Cell _____

Name_____
Address _____
_____
Phone _____
Cell _____

Name_____
Address _____
_____
Phone _____
Cell _____

N

Name_____
Address _____
_____
Phone _____
Cell _____

Name_____
Address _____
_____
Phone _____
Cell _____

Name_____
Address _____
_____
Phone _____
Cell _____

N

Name_____
Address _____
_____
Phone _____
Cell _____

Name_____
Address _____
_____
Phone _____
Cell _____

Name_____
Address _____
_____
Phone _____
Cell _____

N

Name_____
Address _____
_____
Phone _____
Cell _____

Name_____
Address _____
_____
Phone _____
Cell _____

Name_____
Address _____
_____
Phone _____
Cell _____

N

Name_____

Address _____

_____

Phone _____

Cell _____

Name_____

Address _____

_____

Phone _____

Cell _____

Name_____

Address _____

_____

Phone _____

Cell _____

Name_____

Address _____

_____

Phone _____

Cell _____

Name_____

Address _____

_____

Phone _____

Cell _____

Name_____

Address _____

_____

Phone _____

Cell _____

Name_____
Address _____
_____
Phone _____
Cell _____

Name_____
Address _____
_____
Phone _____
Cell _____

Name_____
Address _____
_____
Phone _____
Cell _____

Name _____
Address _____
_____
Phone _____
Cell _____

Name _____
Address _____
_____
Phone _____
Cell _____

Name _____
Address _____
_____
Phone _____
Cell _____

Name_____
Address _____
_____
Phone _____
Cell _____

Name_____
Address _____
_____
Phone _____
Cell _____

Name_____
Address _____
_____
Phone _____
Cell _____

Name _____
Address _____

_____
Phone _____
Cell _____

Name _____
Address _____

_____
Phone _____
Cell _____

Name _____
Address _____

_____
Phone _____
Cell _____

Name_____
Address _____
_____
Phone _____
Cell _____

Name_____
Address _____
_____
Phone _____
Cell _____

Name_____
Address _____
_____
Phone _____
Cell _____

P

Name_____
Address _____
_____
Phone _____
Cell _____

Name_____
Address _____
_____
Phone _____
Cell _____

Name_____
Address _____
_____
Phone _____
Cell _____

P

Name_____
Address _____
_____
Phone _____
Cell _____

Name_____
Address _____
_____
Phone _____
Cell _____

Name_____
Address _____
_____
Phone _____
Cell _____

P

Name_____
Address _____
_____
Phone _____
Cell _____

Name_____
Address _____
_____
Phone _____
Cell _____

Name_____
Address _____
_____
Phone _____
Cell _____

P

Name_____
Address _____
_____
Phone _____
Cell _____

Name_____
Address _____
_____
Phone _____
Cell _____

Name_____
Address _____
_____
Phone _____
Cell _____

P

Name_____
Address _____
_____
Phone _____
Cell _____

Name_____
Address _____
_____
Phone _____
Cell _____

Name_____
Address _____
_____
Phone _____
Cell _____

P

Name_____
Address _____
_____
Phone _____
Cell _____

Name_____
Address _____
_____
Phone _____
Cell _____

Name_____
Address _____
_____
Phone _____
Cell _____

Name_____
Address _____
_____
Phone _____
Cell _____

Name_____
Address _____
_____
Phone _____
Cell _____

Name_____
Address _____
_____
Phone _____
Cell _____

Name_____
Address _____
_____
Phone _____
Cell _____

Name_____
Address _____
_____
Phone _____
Cell _____

Name_____
Address _____
_____
Phone _____
Cell _____

R

Name_____
Address _____
_____
Phone _____
Cell _____

Name_____
Address _____
_____
Phone _____
Cell _____

Name_____
Address _____
_____
Phone _____
Cell _____

R

Name_____
Address _____
_____
Phone _____
Cell _____

Name_____
Address _____
_____
Phone _____
Cell _____

Name_____
Address _____
_____
Phone _____
Cell _____

Name_____

Address _____

_____

Phone _____

Cell _____

Name_____

Address _____

_____

Phone _____

Cell _____

Name_____

Address _____

_____

Phone _____

Cell _____

R

Name_____
Address _____
_____
Phone _____
Cell _____

Name_____
Address _____
_____
Phone _____
Cell _____

Name_____
Address _____
_____
Phone _____
Cell _____

R

Name _____
Address _____
_____
Phone _____
Cell _____

Name _____
Address _____
_____
Phone _____
Cell _____

Name _____
Address _____
_____
Phone _____
Cell _____

R

Name_____
Address _____
_____
Phone _____
Cell _____

Name_____
Address _____
_____
Phone _____
Cell _____

Name_____
Address _____
_____
Phone _____
Cell _____

Name_____
Address _____
_____
Phone _____
Cell _____

Name_____
Address _____
_____
Phone _____
Cell _____

Name_____
Address _____
_____
Phone _____
Cell _____

Name_____
Address _____
_____
Phone _____
Cell _____

Name_____
Address _____
_____
Phone _____
Cell _____

Name_____
Address _____
_____
Phone _____
Cell _____

Name_____
Address _____
_____
Phone _____
Cell _____

Name_____
Address _____
_____
Phone _____
Cell _____

Name_____
Address _____
_____
Phone _____
Cell _____

Name_____
Address _____

_____
Phone _____
Cell _____

Name_____
Address _____

_____
Phone _____
Cell _____

Name_____
Address _____

_____
Phone _____
Cell _____

Name_____
Address _____
_____
Phone _____
Cell _____

Name_____
Address _____
_____
Phone _____
Cell _____

Name_____
Address _____
_____
Phone _____
Cell _____

S

Name_____
Address _____
_____
Phone _____
Cell _____

Name_____
Address _____
_____
Phone _____
Cell _____

Name_____
Address _____
_____
Phone _____
Cell _____

T

Name_____
Address _____
_____
Phone _____
Cell _____

Name_____
Address _____
_____
Phone _____
Cell _____

Name_____
Address _____
_____
Phone _____
Cell _____

T

Name_____
Address _____
_____
Phone _____
Cell _____

Name_____
Address _____
_____
Phone _____
Cell _____

Name_____
Address _____
_____
Phone _____
Cell _____

T

Name_____
Address _____
_____
Phone _____
Cell _____

Name_____
Address _____
_____
Phone _____
Cell _____

Name_____
Address _____
_____
Phone _____
Cell _____

T

Name_____

Address _____

_____

Phone _____

Cell _____

Name_____

Address _____

_____

Phone _____

Cell _____

Name_____

Address _____

_____

Phone _____

Cell _____

T

Name_____
Address _____
_____
Phone _____
Cell _____

Name_____
Address _____
_____
Phone _____
Cell _____

Name_____
Address _____
_____
Phone _____
Cell _____

T

Name_____
Address _____
_____
Phone _____
Cell _____

Name_____
Address _____
_____
Phone _____
Cell _____

Name_____
Address _____
_____
Phone _____
Cell _____

U

Name_____
Address _____
_____
Phone _____
Cell _____

Name_____
Address _____
_____
Phone _____
Cell _____

Name_____
Address _____
_____
Phone _____
Cell _____

U

Name _____

Address _____

_____

Phone _____

Cell _____

Name _____

Address _____

_____

Phone _____

Cell _____

Name _____

Address _____

_____

Phone _____

Cell _____

Name_____
Address _____
_____
Phone _____
Cell _____

Name_____
Address _____
_____
Phone _____
Cell _____

Name_____
Address _____
_____
Phone _____
Cell _____

Name_____
Address _____
_____
Phone _____
Cell _____

Name_____
Address _____
_____
Phone _____
Cell _____

Name_____
Address _____
_____
Phone _____
Cell _____

Name_____
Address _____
_____
Phone _____
Cell _____

Name_____
Address _____
_____
Phone _____
Cell _____

Name_____
Address _____
_____
Phone _____
Cell _____

Name_____
Address _____
_____
Phone _____
Cell _____

Name_____
Address _____
_____
Phone _____
Cell _____

Name_____
Address _____
_____
Phone _____
Cell _____

Name_____
Address _____
_____
Phone _____
Cell _____

Name_____
Address _____
_____
Phone _____
Cell _____

Name_____
Address _____
_____
Phone _____
Cell _____

Name_____
Address _____
_____
Phone _____
Cell _____

Name_____
Address _____
_____
Phone _____
Cell _____

Name_____
Address _____
_____
Phone _____
Cell _____

Name_____
Address _____
_____
Phone _____
Cell _____

Name_____
Address _____
_____
Phone _____
Cell _____

Name_____
Address _____
_____
Phone _____
Cell _____

Name_____
Address _____
_____
Phone _____
Cell _____

Name_____
Address _____
_____
Phone _____
Cell _____

Name_____
Address _____
_____
Phone _____
Cell _____

Name_____
Address _____
_____
Phone _____
Cell _____

Name_____
Address _____
_____
Phone _____
Cell _____

Name_____
Address _____
_____
Phone _____
Cell _____

Name_____
Address _____
_____
Phone _____
Cell _____

Name_____
Address _____
_____
Phone _____
Cell _____

Name_____
Address _____
_____
Phone _____
Cell _____

Z

Name_____

Address _____

_____

Phone _____

Cell _____

Name_____

Address _____

_____

Phone _____

Cell _____

Name_____

Address _____

_____

Phone _____

Cell _____

Z

Name_____

Address _____

_____

Phone _____

Cell _____

Name_____

Address _____

_____

Phone _____

Cell _____

Name_____

Address _____

_____

Phone _____

Cell _____

NOTES

NOTES

NOTES

NOTES

CPSIA information can be obtained
at www.ICGtesting.com
Printed in the USA
BVOW04s1323051217
502028BV00015B/94/P